FORGIVENESS

Gardens of the Heart

FORGIVENESS

ELIZABETH CLARE PROPHET

SUMMIT UNIVERSITY PRESS®

GARDINER, MONTANA

FORGIVENESS
by Elizabeth Clare Prophet
Copyright © 2012 Summit Publications, Inc.
All rights reserved

For information, contact Summit University Press,
63 Summit Way, Gardiner, MT 59030.
Tel: 1-800-245-5445 or 406-848-9500
www.SummitUniversityPress.com

Library of Congress Control Number 2012931433
ISBN 978-1-60988-069-9
ISBN 978-1-60988-103-0 (eBook)

SUMMIT UNIVERSITY 🔥 PRESS®
Summit University Press and 🔥 are trademarks registered in the U.S. Patent and Trademark Office and in other countries. All rights reserved.

Cover and interior design by James Bennett Design

Printed in the United States of America
16 15 14 13 12   5 4 3 2 1

CONTENTS

Approaching the Garden

Forgiveness has the power to transform your life and heal wounds of the heart and mind. Let forgiveness become a part of your day and enjoy a profound freedom from stress, anxiety, and painful memories.

As you forgive yourself, you will be able to forgive others. As you forgive others, you will be forgiven.

Forgiveness is forgetting the wrong, because you have made it irrelevant and it has no more power over you.

You never know what hardships a person is facing or the pain that burdens them. When you forgive them, you withhold judgment of any kind, lifting the burden of condemnation. That single act of forgiveness can give them the grace to change and transform their life.

Without forgiveness, you create an image of the one who hurt you and you give that image the power to damage, destroy, and offend you. With forgiveness, you can have absolute freedom from the past.

A Ritual of Forgiveness that you may wish to use or modify for your needs has been included at the back of the book.

We encourage your daily walk through the garden of your heart.

THE ARBOR

Forgiveness

as a quality of the heart

benefits the forgiver

more than the forgiven.

Be gracious with forgiveness.

You never know the burden

another is carrying,

so forgive again and again.

Start each new season

by forgiving yourself

for all wrongs, all infractions.

Be willing to exercise

all the ingenuity of your heart

to bring about genuine

forgiveness and resolution.

Forgiveness

is not something that many

take upon themselves or give to others.

But forgive again and again

and again and again

because you know not

what is burdening another,

even one seated next to you

or in just another room.

Without love,

there is no forgiveness.

Without forgiveness,

there is no moving on.

Seek forgiveness

from all you have wronged.

Pour forgiveness without limit

upon all who have wronged you.

The road to resolution

and inner peace

goes through forgiveness.

Let forgiveness for errors flow

to others and to yourself as well.

Let forgiveness bring renewal

until, like the sunrise,

it glows upon the horizon

of the world.

When you feel love for someone,

you are more willing

to ask that one's forgiveness.

Cultivate the love that brings

resolution through forgiveness.

Why do people need forgiveness?

Because people make mistakes.

Is there anyone on earth

who has not made a mistake?

Bear to all a heart

full of love and forgiveness.

Forgiveness

is the mark of love,

ultimate love.

And it is the forgetting

with the forgiving

that is the mark of forgiveness.

Forgiveness contains the power

to bring change and healing.

May you give to all

the understanding

that there is forgiveness.

Never hold onto or recite

another's past or present faults.

Hold no concept of another

that is less than the perfection

of that one's real self.

Keep a pad next to your nightstand
and write down those who come to
mind whom you have not forgiven.
Find them. Ask for forgiveness.

Start each day afresh.

Forgive and be willing

to receive forgiveness.

Bear the balm of forgiveness

and give it to all who suffer.

THE LILY POND

To be able to forgive others,

forgive yourself first.

Through acts of forgiveness,

strive for the perfecting

of your heart.

Have the humility to know

that you need forgiveness.

It's not easy to say

I'm sorry, I was wrong.

Feel humble sorrow

for wrongdoing

but hold to the assured hope

that genuine repentance

will lead to forgiveness and pardon.

Clothed in forgiveness,

life becomes easier.

Ponder what it would mean

for your life to have

mercy and forgiveness

as a trailing garment

with you always.

Ask forgiveness, make amends,

and determine not to make

the same mistake again.

The way to avoid backsliding

is to feel sincere regret for error

and to feel genuine love

for every part of life.

Often the hardest person

to forgive is yourself.

If you are burdened with guilt,

you cannot move on.

Open your heart to forgiveness.

You have the capacity

to remove pain,

to bring forgiveness,

to bring surcease.

Run to the one

you have wronged and say,

"Forgive me

and let us walk on the road of life

together."

Welcome forgiveness

as a river of cleansing,

a river of affection,

a river of life.

We have all done things

that we are not proud of,

so forgive the human condition.

The way to inner harmony

is through mercy and forgiveness

whereby you forgive yourself

and you forgive others.

Whatever your mistakes were,

you were doing the best

you could at the time.

It is time to forgive yourself

and keep your eye focused

on the vast potential

that is inside of you.

Through forgiveness,

see each day as a fresh start

in which to lay

new guidelines to becoming

who and what you want to be.

Is not the forgiveness of a friend

one of the greatest gifts

you can ever receive—

that someone has loved you

enough to forgive you?

Some of the most precious

moments in life may be those

in which you receive

profound forgiveness

from someone you respect.

People make mistakes

until they have the experience

and discrimination

to make better choices.

As you take responsibility

for errors made along the way,

forgive yourself and move on.

Open yourself to forgiveness.

Embrace gentle forgiveness

like a prodigal son returning

to the heart of his father.

Learn to forgive yourself for error

and learn to accept the love

your heart craves.

Forgiveness comes to you

through efforts to make amends

and right past wrongs.

Forgiveness is sustained

by continuing right action.

A VIOLET-
PINK ROSE

A violet-pink rose

with depth of hue

and color,

a rose of love

and forgiveness.

Have a heart

filled with love

and forgiveness.

Ponder your life and consider

how you can achieve resolution.

Can you forgive God?

Forgive gratefully

and generously.

Some wrongs and crimes burn

so profoundly and deeply that

they are hard to forgive.

The secret is to forgive

the soul and inner identity

of the one that has done wrong.

If you can forgive the soul,

a wonderful freedom awaits you.

If you feel vengeance for someone

because they have wronged you,

let it go. Let God take care of it.

As long as you hold resentment,

you are bound to that person.

To be healed of the scar,

forgive the wrong.

Free yourself through love

and compassion.

Justice belongs to the Creator;

it is the Creator's province.

Therefore, there is justice

for wrongdoing.

But forgiveness belongs to you.

Your province is to forgive

and forgive again.

May you be blessed

with the fragrance

of the violets of forgiveness.

Give the cup of forgiveness

to others and you will discover

an astounding relief

from burdens you have

carried for so long.

Give the cup of forgiveness

and discover

an astounding transmutation.

Feeling anger or resentment

when a past wrong comes to mind

is a signal that you have yet

to extend forgiveness.

When you let go of grudges

and truly forgive life,

the energy you send forth

comes flowing back to you

as floodtides of forgiveness

in your own life.

Be wholly active in giving

and receiving forgiveness.

See how many problems

can be resolved through

mercy and forgiveness.

The fragrance of lilacs and violets

speaks of eternal springtime.

Springtime speaks to the heart

of forgiveness and renewal.

Let the rivers and waters run

with the wine of forgiveness.

Mercy is the quality of nobility

within you that loves,

exalts, and forgives.

We need forgiveness

in relationships.

We all have much to forgive

and much to be forgiven for.

Utter the word of forgiveness

to every single, solitary heart.

Let your heart become

a seat of mercy

where forgiveness dwells.

Forgive,

because forgiveness frees us.

Hatred is binding.

Non-forgiveness is enslaving.

In the end,

if we do not forgive,

we become the prisoners

of our non-forgiveness.

It will bring you great joy

to simply give forgiveness.

HERBS

By forgiveness we heal.

Forgiveness dissolves hatreds,

the desire for revenge.

Forgiveness

is the gift of flowing freedom,

of joy, of happiness,

of transcendent, buoyant resilience

that looks into the very teeth

of error and declares,

"You have no power over me!"

Forgiveness

is the beginning

of healing.

The antidotes to many diseases

begin in the mind—

with good humor, joy,

love, compassion,

and forgiveness.

Know you not

that when you forgive another

and thereby free that one

from bondage

it is in reality you yourself

who is freed?

To forgive another

and to ask forgiveness

takes surrender

of the desire to be right.

Accept

the need for forgiveness.

Ask for it.

Gentle forgiveness...

The magnanimous heart

does not withhold

the gentle, comforting word

of uplift or forgiveness.

Forgiveness flows from the fount

of a magnanimous heart.

Open up your heart

and give loving forgiveness

again and again and again.

It is by love

that healing comes forth—

and love begins with forgiveness.

If you desire to put behind you

the wrongs you have done,

be willing to forgive the wrongs

others have done unto you.

If you have not forgiven

a person or a situation,

you tend to re-create it.

In order to heal fully

from a wrong, forgive fully.

Pray for comfort to envelop

those you have wronged.

Pray to clear up misunderstandings

and for the healing of all harm.

Pray for a softening of hearts,

that all may forgive and move on.

Forgiveness is a choice

to let go of resentment

and to release the memory

of any wrongdoing.

The effects of forgiveness

go far beyond the forgiving

of a debt or a wrong.

Forgiveness is a supportive love

that comes from attunement

with the heart and results in

a more perfect love being received

by the one forgiven.

We receive forgiveness

in like measure

as we forgive others.

This is a universal truth.

The balm of forgiveness

carries the potential to soften

even a hardened heart.

Speak healing words of forgiveness

to everyone, to every heart.

Forgiveness is a quality of the heart

that benefits the one who forgives

more than the one forgiven.

When you truly forgive,

you free yourself from the image

of the one to whom you had given

the power to hurt or harm you

or in any way offend you.

Look upon wrongs done to you

as opportunities

to learn forgiveness,

to learn about yourself,

and to be more the master

of your life.

Sometimes people hold a grudge

for a perceived wrong

when the reality is

that they misunderstood

another's motive or actions.

Take every opportunity

to forgive any and all.

Forgive every part of life.

Love every part of life.

This results in a true

healing of the soul,

even at the level

of the unconscious.

A SWING
FOR TWO

Let a gentle rain of forgiveness

renew your heart.

Some people

will never forget a wrong

that has been done to them though they

may forget

the wrongs they have done

to others.

Without love,

there is no forgiveness.

Without forgiveness,

there is no forgetfulness.

Forgiveness heals.

Give forgiveness

with great joy in your heart.

Let mercy and forgiveness

be amplified for all life

that the beauty of the world

as the Creator made it

might blossom fully

in the consciousness of all.

Every soul on earth needs

the assistance and polishing

that comes through forgiveness.

We all need forgiveness,

because we all get involved

in some outer turmoil

as we walk the road of life.

The tender, forgiving love

that binds together

the members of a family

is the same forgiving love

that binds the wounds

of the nations.

Let forgiveness expand

over the earth

as wings of healing joy.

Forgiveness

is the evergreen that enfolds the earth,

that adorns the children,

that weaves a flower in the hair

of the young mother

and the young child.

Forgive and ask to be forgiven—

even if you think you were right.

Do it to forgive another.

Do it so another has

an opportunity to forgive you.

Live by the code of forgiveness.

Forgiveness gives fresh opportunity

to use life's energies correctly.

Let every unkind thought

and act of non-forgiveness

fly out of the cage of your being.

Free the energy that has bound you.

Begin and end each day

with forgiveness

of yourself and others.

Are you willing

to forgive yourself

for your errors?

Start out today and tomorrow

and every day as long as you live

to forgive yourself

and forgive people.

Don't be afraid to forgive.

To forgive is divine.

Live each day

as if it were your last.

Forgive, be kind, and speak

words of comfort to all.

Angels

attend

you...

A Ritual of Forgiveness

Close your eyes and let the events of the day pass before you like a movie. Call to mind the people who need your love and forgiveness. Silently in your heart or in spoken prayer, forgive each situation and person, and ask forgiveness for your part.

See a blazing violet fire passing through the scenes in your mind. Watch the flames neutralize any negative impact of the day's events. Pray for resolution and inner peace, and send healing thoughts to all concerned, yourself included.

Focus your attention on your heart. Send love and forgiveness to anyone you have wronged and to all who have wronged you. Release each scene, each memory, each situation to your own higher self and the higher self of the other person.

Letting go of any sense of injustice, anger, or guilt by the end of each day will set you on the road to better health, inner peace, and true happiness.

Gardens of the Heart Series

Compassion

Gratitude

Forgiveness

Joy

Jardines del corazón

Compasión

Gratitud

Perdón

Alegría

For other titles by
Elizabeth Clare Prophet,
please visit

www.SummitUniversityPress.com